HANSON

FOREVER

Your TAY, ZAC, and IKE Keepsake Scrapbook

SCHOLASTIC INC.

NEW YORK   TORONTO   LONDON   AUCKLAND   SYDNEY   MEXICO CITY   NEW DELHI   HONG KONG

Photography credits:
Cover: Derrick Santini/ESP; back cover: Derrick Santini/ESP; page 3: APRF/Shooting Star; 4: Derrick Santini/ESP; 5: Derrick Santini/ESP; 6: Derrick Santini/ESP; 8: Evan Agostini/Gamma Liaison; 9: APRF/Shooting Star; 10, top: Eddie Malluk; 10, bottom: Steve Granitz/Retna; 11: Eddie Malluk; 12, top: Melanie Edwards/Retna; 12, bottom: Anthony Cutajar/London Features; 14: Derrick Santini/ESP; 15: Celebrity Photo Agency; 16: Celebrity Photo Agency; 17, left: Ron Wolfson/London Features; 17, right: Ernie Paniccioli/Retna; 18: Jon Mead/Star File Photo; 19: Derrick Santini/ESP; 19, inset: Eddie Malluk; 20: Derrick Santini/ESP; 21, top: Steve Granitz/Retna; 21, bottom: Ernie Paniccioli/Retna; 22, top: Ernie Paniccioli/Retna; 22, bottom: Sean Murphy/Camera Press/Retna; 23: Ernie Paniccioli/Retna; 24: Derrick Santini/ESP; 25, top: APRF/Shooting Star; 25, bottom: Celebrity Photo Agency; 26: Derrick Santini/ESP; 27: Ron Wolfson/London Features; 27, inset: Ernie Paniccioli/Retna; 28: David Atlas/Retna; 29, left: Eddie Malluk; 29, right: Ron Wolfson/London Features; 30: APRF/Shooting Star; 31: Ernie Paniccioli/Retna; 32, top: Ernie Paniccioli/Retna; 32, bottom: Celebrity Photo Agency; 33: APRF/Shooting Star; 34, top: Nick Elgar/London Features; 34, bottom: Ron Wolfson/London Features; 35, top: Eddie Malluk; 35, bottom: David Atlas/Retna; 36, top left: Ron Wolfson/London Features; 36, top right: Celebrity Photo Agency; 36, bottom: Celebrity Photo Agency; 38, top left: Jon Mead/Star File Photo; 38, top right: Dennis Van Tine/London Features; 38, bottom: Ron Wolfson/London Features; 39: Derrick Santini/ESP; 40: Barry King/Gamma Liaison; 41: Larry Busacca/Retna; 42: Youri Lenquette/Retna; 43, top: Larry Busacca/Retna; 43, bottom: Ron Wolfson/London Features; 44: Derrick Santini/ESP; 45: Janet Gough/Celebrity Photo Agency; 46, top: Eric Catarina/Retna; 46, bottom: Ernie Paniccioli/Retna; 47, top: Jon Mead/Star File Photo; 47, bottom: Evan Agostini/Gamma Liaison; 48: Derrick Santini/ESP.

ISBN 0-439-04530-4

12 11 10 9 8 7 6 5 4 3 2 1   8 9/9 0 1 2 3/0

Printed in the U.S.A.

First Scholastic printing, September 1998

Welcome to HANSON FOREVER!

Give yourself snaps for picking up this scrapbook. It's the one you'll use now, *and* it's the one you'll come back to, time and again. Why? Check the title: **Your Keepsake Scrapbook**. Like any **SCRAPBOOK**, first and foremost, it's plastered with Hanson photos and info-obsessed captions, bearing the latest, hottest 411 on the brotherly band.

Then there's the **KEEPSAKE** part. In most chapters, there's space for you to record your feelings, your memories, maybe even some of your favorite Hanson snapshots and souvenirs.

Then there's that word, **FOREVER**. Will you really love Hanson forever? Who knows? But one day, you will look back on the time you did. That's when you'll dig this scrapbook out of the attic, the bottom drawer, back of the closet, wherever you stashed it. And the minute you open it, it will remind you of exactly how you feel about **TAYLOR, ZAC**, and **IKE HANSON** right this moment.

WHAT'S INSIDE

REWIND — THE BACK STORY

The Hanson story is equal parts love, dedication, vision, hard work, devotion, and a whole lot of music. Above all else, it's a family story.

It takes place in the heartland of the USA, Tulsa, Oklahoma, and grows from the love of two very special people, Walker and Diana Lawyer Hanson. The pair met at Nathan Hale High School and struck an instant rapport. Both native Tulsans, they shared many values, including unshakable spirituality, a strong work ethic, and a love of music. Walker played guitar; Diana, a music major at the University of Oklahoma, once sang with the Horizons, a gospel group that performed all over the country.

When they married and started a family, all those beliefs and all that innate talent were firmly in place. Their kids inherited it all.

The first three were boys, called Isaac, Taylor, and Zac. Music filled their lives from the get go. To the strains of their dad's guitar at bedtime, the trio of lookalike tykes would sing. Their natural harmonies, still untrained and unaffected, were beautiful.

They learned the songs their parents taught them, and before long, without prompting, were making up their own ditties, some silly, some serious. At dinnertime, they'd sing around the table. As they grew, music was the soundtrack to which they'd do their chores, their homework, watch TV, play games. When Walker's job transported the clan to South America for a year, music came with them, influenced them, and eventually planted the earliest seeds of . . . **THE DREAM.**

At first, the dream was modest. They simply wanted to share their amazing harmonies with others. To that end, dressed in matching outfits, they'd perform *a cappella* (without music) at picnics and parties run by the company where their dad worked. The reaction to the trilling trio was off the hook. Everyone was amazed by their sweet, soulful sounds, and inherently beautiful harmonies.

RANDOM FACT: Their earliest identical stage outfits included matching flowered Hawaiian shirts, denim jackets, and button-down white shirts with bow ties.

And then, the dream grew. As word of Ike, Tay, and Zac's talent spread through town, they were invited to perform at more events. The demand grew, and the boys reacted by putting a stage act together, complete with rudimentary choreography and between-songs patter. They'd perform harmonic renditions of songs everyone knows — a little old-time rock 'n' roll, a few gospel tunes, some soul music too. Little by little, they added their own originals to the mix. By the time Ike was twelve, the brothers had hundreds of Hanson originals to pick from.

It grew . . . and grew . . . Learning to play instruments was the next step, and the boys dove into it wholeheartedly. Guitar had always been Ike's passion, and handily, Walker was around to teach him. Tay took to keyboards like a little fish to water. And who else to pound the skins but irrepressible Zac? It all fit.

And finally, the dream took shape and blossomed. As a family, and as a music group, Hanson began to realize that singing, writing, and performing was like a calling: something they not only loved doing, but wanted and needed to do. Their creativity was blossoming, and reaction to the band was spreading way beyond Tulsa city limits.

And they worked it — to the max. Hanson played everywhere and anywhere. They never felt "too good" for any venue that invited them. They played elementary school assemblies, amusement parks, water parks, county fairs, state fairs, ball games, local Tulsa music events like Mayfest, even backyard barbecues and block parties. Sometimes they didn't even get paid. But they did ask for, and receive, other means of compensation. Hanson created T-shirts and souvenirs and made money by selling those at their earliest concerts. When they invested their own money and recorded their earliest CDs (*Boomerang* and *MMMBop*), they set up a booth and sold those at concerts, too. In some instances, they asked for, and received, names and addresses of audience members, from which they compiled a mailing list. Those fans would receive word of any new Hanson performance.

And then ... YESSSS! ... the dream came true. It is said that dreams become reality when opportunity meets preparedness. Hanson are living proof. In addition to the dues-paying gigs, years of writing, rehearsing, and learning their instruments, they sent demo tapes of their songs to record companies. Most sent rejection notes, but one day, one didn't. Instead, Mercury Records came to see them perform at a state fair.

Soon the band was signed, sent to L.A. to record their first album, *Middle of Nowhere*. And ... MMMBop! the rest is history.

The über-FAQ [most frequently asked question]: "What's 'MMMBop' about?"

REWIND: YOUR BACK STORY
Fill in Your Own Hanson Memories.

How I First Heard About Hanson:_____

How Old I Was:_____

Where I First Saw Hanson (on TV, in concert):
_____

My First Reaction to
"MMMBop":_____

The Hanson I Liked Best Was:_____

My Favorite Hanson Song from Middle of Nowhere:
_____

My Friend Who Loved Them:
_____

Clip Your First Favorite Hanson Picture Here:

Chapter Two

SAY HEY, TAY!

His birth certificate lists him as "Jordan Taylor Hanson." On CDs and official showbiz stuff, it's Taylor. But to everyone who loves him — family, friends, and fans — it's Tay.

He's the family's second-born son, the one with the easily flushed cheeks, sexy curl to his upper lip, intense blue eyes, and shy smile. He's the keyboard player, tambourine man, and on most songs, lead singer.

Tay is also the reluctant heartthrob, the one who inspires the loudest screams at concerts, the most banners, Web sites, and is on fan mail overload. He's flattered, of course, yet he doesn't revel in it. Truthful Tay admits that being singled out embarrasses him. He tries never to pose alone, but always with his brothers, and does nothing to encourage the adoration. He honestly, genuinely feels that the entire band, and their support system (family, friends, backup musicians) all deserve the same credit and attention.

That's the kind of dude Taylor is. He's also funny, sensitive, confident — and even though he's not the oldest, in many ways, he's the leader.

Taylorisms:

"Busy streak," instead of busy period or creative streak.

"Twisted together," instead of mixed together.

"That's cool!"

"Weird!"

RANDOM FACT: Isn't it weird? The only "official" book about Hanson doesn't have one single chapter on their personalities, private lives, what they like and dislike. It's a musical history of the group.

TAYLOR TOP TO TOE

Birthday: March 14, 1983

Zodiac Sign: Pisces

Birthplace: Jenks, Oklahoma

Grew Up In: Tulsa, Oklahoma

Height: 5'8"

Weight: 125 lbs.

Hair Color: Blond

Eye Color: Blue

ALL ABOUT ME

Birthday:_____

Zodiac Sign:_____

Birthplace:_____

Grew Up In:_____

Height:_____

Weight:_____

Hair Color:_____

Eye Color:_____

TAY'S FAVORITES

Colors: Blue, red
TV Show: *Frasier, Friends, Animaniacs*
Music: The Motown sound
Actor: Tom Cruise
Actress: Jennifer Aniston
Sports Team: Miami Dolphins
Movie: *Star Wars*
Game: Laser Quest
Store: The Gap
Food: Burritos, steak, cheeseburgers

MY FAVORITES

Colors:_____
TV Show:_____
_____
Music:_____
Actor:_____
Actress:_____
Sports Team:_____
_____
Movie:_____
Game:_____
Store:_____
Food:_____

RANDOM FACT: That fabric flower in the "MMMBop" video? It's now on the garage wall at home in Tulsa.

Taylor Quotes

On Hansonmania: "You can't help liking it."

On Music: "I always knew I loved it and that it was a part of me."

On Success: "When you want something, you have to work for it."

Ten Things TAY Loves:

1. Animals
2. The Jackson 5. "They rocked," says Tay.
3. Drawing pictures of dinosaurs and band members
4. Writing in his journal
5. Rollerblading
6. Wearing lots of chokers at once
7. Doc Martens shoes and boots
8. Creamy peanut butter
9. Surfing the Net
10. "That people all over the world like our music. That's the most awesome thing of all."

Ten Things I Love:

1._____
2._____
3._____
4._____
5._____
6._____
7._____
8._____
9._____
10._____

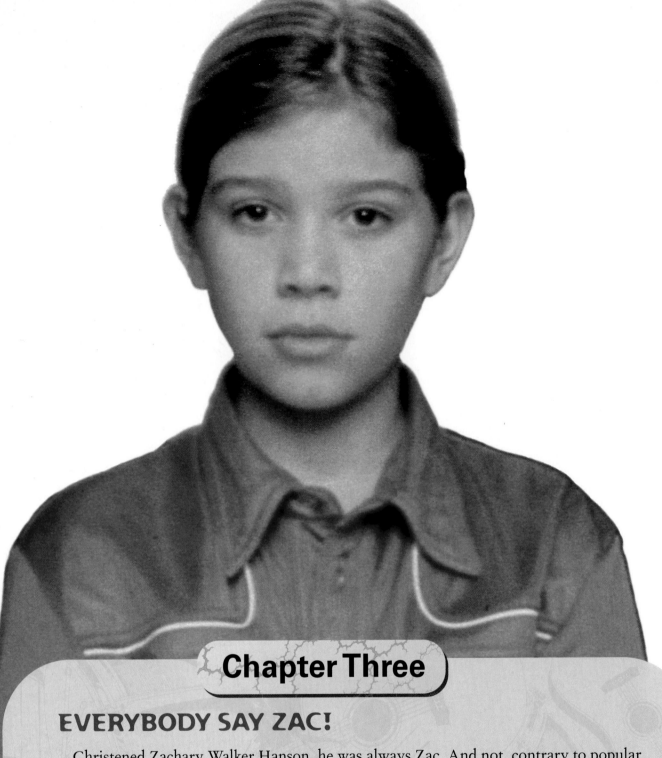

Chapter Three

EVERYBODY SAY ZAC!

Christened Zachary Walker Hanson, he was always Zac. And not, contrary to popular legend, because it rhymes with "attack"!

He may be the youngest, but in many ways, Zac is the center of planet Hanson. Much revolves around him, and if it doesn't? Just give him a minute. Hanson's own little drummer boy is an unabashed attention animal, the one who can't sit still, or keep still. "Quips R Zac," and no matter what anyone says to squash them, they just keep on coming. But

Zac's natural ebullience and lack of pretense keep him firmly on the positive side of charming.

It's easy to dismiss Zac as the family ham, or as one bruised reporter (caught in a Zac attack) dubbed him, "MMMBrat," but neither is fair. For Zac is way more complicated than that. He's the sharpie who always looks out for Hanson's image. In an early interview, even before "MMMBop" changed everything, it was Zac who put the kibosh on certain questions *he* didn't consider appropriate! And he's the boy who still loves playing with his Power Rangers and drawing in crayon, who sticks most to his musical guns when issues erupt during recording sessions. He's rock 'n' roll's youngest professional drummer. He pulls his weight musically and his opinions carry great weight within Hanson Inc.

Besides, Zac isn't truly unruly. There is a quiet, sensitive side to the young teenager. Once, he alluded to the pressure of maintaining that hyper image. "If I'm serious, people say, 'What's the matter? Is it a bad day for you?'" In quiet moments, Zac gets thoughtful and creative. He's an awesome artist who can sit for hours, designing his own comic books or just thinking. Zac really is all that — and a bag of chips.

ZAC WAY BACK: He wasn't all that different than he is now. An eyewitness to one of Hanson's early concerts at the Blue Rose Café recalls (in Hanson's official bio), "Zac would make all sorts of strange noises between songs. He looked like he wanted to jump up from behind his drum kit, run off, and do something else."

"Our mom wanted to home-school us because she wanted to have a closer relationship with us." — Zac, according to Hanson: The Official Book

ZAC & You: The Hookup

What Scares ZAC:

1. Getting mobbed by fans, especially when no one's around to rescue him.
2. Strangers
3. Reporters who ask weird questions

What Scares Me:

1.
2.
3.

Zac Describes Himself:

1. "Goofy-stupid"
2. "Singer/songwriter"
3. A math whiz

I Describe Myself:

1.
2.
3.

ZAC FACT PACK

Birthday: October 22, 1985
Nickname: "Animal," after the Muppet drummer
Zodiac Sign: Libra
Instruments: Drums, mini-maracas
Hair Color: Blond
Eye Color: Brown
Height: 5'3"
Weight: 100 lbs.
In School: Zac, like his brothers, is home-schooled. He's in the equivalent of seventh grade.

ZAC'S FAVORITES

Music: Spin Doctors, Counting Crows, Aerosmith
TV Show: Cartoons
Movies: Action movies like *Twister* and *Total Recall*
Food: If Zac could start with dessert, he would. He loves all flavors of Jell-O, and chocolate ice cream.
Clothes: Loud!
Shoes: Zac boasts a collection of Doc Martens
Sports: Skateboarding, basketball, soccer
Color: Blue

QUIBBLES & BITS
A Roundup of Recently Printed Zac Quotes

"I cannot betray a song. We love all the songs [we sing]. They're all too valuable."
"D'oh!" (like Homer Simpson)
"Ding Dongs and Twinkies are my most important food group."
"Tay and Ike are like my best friends, only bester."

Chapter Four

EYE ON IKE!

His birth certificate lists the first-born Hanson hottie as Clarke Isaac. In the biz, he's Isaac, but everyone calls him Ike. Easy to like, less easy to get to know, Ike has been called Hanson's true musical historian and purest artist, the rhythmic center of the group.

Ike is the most pragmatic member of the band, the least likely to let fame swell his head. "All this [acclaim] can go just as fast as it came," is not only his oft-printed quote, but his philosophy.

If Ike comes across as self-confident, it's no cover-up. He is strong-minded, opinionated, and hardly ever waffles or secondguesses himself. He's straightforward, sensible, and ready to tackle even the most difficult challenge. Competition? Disappointment? Bring it on: It just makes him want to work harder.

Loyalty is not only Ike's best trait, it's how he judges others.

YIKES! IKE'S FACT FILE
Birthday: November 17, 1980
Zodiac Sign: Scorpio
Nickname: Chewbacca, compliments of Tay!
Height: 5'10"
Weight: 145 lbs.
Hair Color: Dark blond
Eye Color: Brown
Pet: A turtle
Instrument: Guitar
Favorite Color: Green
Sport: Rollerblading
Food: Steak, lasagna
Fast Food: Domino's pizza
He Admits to Crushin' On: Cindy Crawford

Five Things Ike Is Known For:

1. Doing imitations of cartoon characters
2. Telling jokes
3. Playing long guitar solos
4. His collection of sci-fi books
5. His skill at street hockey

Five Things I'm Known For:

1.
2.
3.
4.
5.

> "If we had girlfriends, we probably wouldn't tell you."
> —Ike (Entertainment Tonight)

Five Things That Bug Ike:

1. Being compared with other bands
2. Being asked personal questions
3. Paparazzi photographers
4. Seeing himself on TV
5. Fingernails on chalkboard

Three Habits He Has:

1. Doing karate kicks with Taylor
2. Making everyone laugh
3. Writing songs. He's been at it since the age of eight.

Five Things That Bug Me:

1.

2.

3.
4.
5.

Three Habits I Have:

1.
2.
3.

Chapter Five

THE SECRETS NO ONE KNOWS

Now, you do.

Everyone knows . . . the boys all took classical piano lessons.
But few know . . . they also took dance lessons.

Everyone knows . . . they got lots of rejections from record companies.
But few know . . . they actually rejected the first — and at the time, the only!! — offer they ever got, on the sound advice that it was a bad deal.

Everyone knows . . . they make the coolest videos.
But few know . . . the first video they made themselves got them roles in a soft drink commercial. How come you never saw it? It was scrapped.

Everyone knows . . . it was when they played at a state fair in Coffeyville, Kansas, that a record company exec flew out to see them, and signed them.
But few know . . . the boys considered it one of their *worst* gigs ever! "We performed well, but the audience really didn't get into it," Tay has revealed.

Everyone knows . . . Zac often sports braids.
But few know . . . Mom often does the honors. It's hard for southpaw Zac.

The dumbest question ever asked: "How'd you guys meet?"

Who's Hanging on the Hanson Family Tree?

Mom: Diana Lawyer Hanson
Dad: Clarke Walker Hanson
Clarke Isaac
Jordan Taylor
Zachary Walker
Jessica
Avery
Mackenzie
And the newest Hanson, Zoe Genvieve, born on
January 14, 1998, at St. John Medical Center in Tulsa.

HANSON PETS:
Ike's turtle
Tay's cat, MaMa

MY FAMILY TREE:
Mom:
Dad:
My Siblings:

MY PETS:

Chapter Six

ROAD WARRIORS

Performing for whomever wants to listen was Hanson's goal from the get go, and in many ways, it still is. Pursuit of that goal has taken Hanson . . . well, as they put it, from Tulsa to Tokyo to the Middle of Nowhere and back 'round again. What's it like being on the road with the Hanson hotties?

Touring, of course, is nothing new to Hanson. In the earliest days, they'd pile in the family van with Dad at the wheel and drive from gig to gig. Sometimes, the rickety van would barely make it from one city to the next — and sometimes, it didn't. During one famous breakdown, while their dad was on repair duty, Zac got the idea for "Man from Milwaukee."

Success has brought many changes for Hanson, not least among them the way they travel. Now, it's first-class, be it on planes or their own fully equipped tour buses.

Even so, the "getting there" part of touring can be a drag, but the Hanson brothers use their down time well. Actually, they kind of have to. That's one place they get schooled. Tutors come along with the guys and go over their lessons. Homework gets done there, too.

At each pit stop, the family and their entourage will check into a hotel that's near the venue. What would you find if you peeked into the rooms of Ike, Tay, and Zac? Well, neatniks they're not. Hotel rooms are proof. "We're messy," conceded Tay.

"Our Doc Martens are scattered all over the rooms," Zac added. He also admits to collecting those complimentary bottles of shampoo.

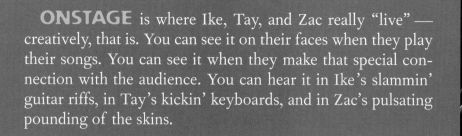

ONSTAGE is where Ike, Tay, and Zac really "live" — creatively, that is. You can see it on their faces when they play their songs. You can see it when they make that special connection with the audience. You can hear it in Ike's slammin' guitar riffs, in Tay's kickin' keyboards, and in Zac's pulsating pounding of the skins.

RANDOM FACT: Hanson's manager, Chris Sabac, used to represent the Dave Matthews Band.

At the airport, Dad Walker (left) is always with them.

A HANSON CONCERT in your town is a not-to-be-missed event. They spent the summer of '98 doing the coast-to-coast thing, then they went overseas.

The Hanson's mom, rarely photographed, makes it a family affair at the airport.

YOUR TURN: WHEN I SAW HANSON IN CONCERT

I saw Hanson in concert in [where?]:_____

I was with [friends, family]:_____

My favorite song they sang was:_____

I remember what they said when they talked to
the audience:_____

_____

_____

What surprised me most about the show was:

_____

_____

_____

I screamed when:_____

_____

I'll remember it always because:

_____

_____

Tay waves to fans from a hotel window.

NAMES THEY'VE BEEN KNOWN BY:
Of course they were always Hanson,
but they weren't always Hanson. Get
it? Early audiences knew them as The
Hanson Brothers. Then, they were
just The Hansons. Now, of course, it's
been trimmed to simply Hanson.

Chapter Seven

PAUSE — IS IT TRUE?

Because Hanson is so popular, people love to talk about them. Often, what "they" say is full-on bogus, but sometimes there is a grain of truth. For instance . . .

RUMOR: "Yearbook" is about kids Hanson really knew.
TRUTH: Since they've been mostly home-schooled, they've never had an actual yearbook. The song sprang from their fertile imaginations — and from the pen of professional songwriter Ellen Shipley, who cowrote it.

RUMOR: Zac's pants were pulled down by crazed fans.
TRUTH: No! But Tay's shirt was once ripped by a feverish fan — who also managed to snare one shoelace.

RUMOR: The boys have been seriously injured by fans.
TRUTH: Luckily, no, but they came close in Asia, where fans pulled their hair. "They were the most aggressive fans, definitely," remembers Tay. "They pounded on the sides of the van and on the windows."

RUMOR: Hanson did a milk mustache commercial.
TRUTH: Who hasn't?

RUMOR: Hanson now live in Los Angeles.
TRUTH: While they consider the "left coast" to be home away from home, the family maintains its main residence in West Tulsa, Oklahoma.

RUMOR: Their younger sibs, Jessica, Avery, and Mackenzie are going to start their own band, to be called Hanson II.
TRUTH: Too cute, but no. At least, there are no plans for that. More likely, if the younger kids show an aptitude for it, they'll join Ike, Tay, and Zac onstage as "guest performers." That's how Janet Jackson began. Really.

RUMOR: Taylor Hanson never wants a girlfriend.
TRUTH: Tay doesn't have time to make a commitment right now, but that's far from "never." Of course he'd like a girlfriend, but it'll be a while before he acts on that desire.

RUMOR: Zac called a reporter a weirdo.
TRUTH: MMM . . . yeah. That was a real Zac attack! It happened backstage at the Nickelodeon Kids' Choice Awards. One reporter asked about the family's religious convictions and got a polite response about that being a private matter. Another reporter, however, wouldn't let it go and continued to pry. That's when Zac burst. "You're a weirdo," is his direct quote. It didn't quite stop there. Another reporter asked how it felt to be a sex symbol at such a young age, and Zac let loose, "Oh, we have another weirdo in the room."

RUMOR: Ike has a crush on Fiona Apple.
TRUTH: Ike and the boys met Fiona Apple backstage in L.A. — that's all.

RUMOR: Hanson is seriously crushing on Jewel.
TRUTH: It was reported in the *New York Post* that backstage at the Grammy Awards, the boys were eyeing and "flirting with" the "Wonder of the Tundra," who was dressed to bedazzle that night.

RUMOR: Hanson won't tour because Ike's going to college.
TRUTH: Ike may one day attend college, but not right now. Making music and singing for fans comes first.

RUMOR: Zac's voice changed.
TRUTH: He's a growing boy, and one day it will. But not quite yet.

RUMOR: Hanson will have a Saturday morning cartoon show.
TRUTH: Hanson have been offered a Saturday morning cartoon show — and a whole lot more — but they turned it down, so no. The boys are concentrating on their music.

RUMOR: Hanson are breaking up.
TRUTH: Okay, they're not the Spice Girls. As Zac has said, "We're brothers. We can't break up." Not only that — they wouldn't want to.

RUMOR: Hanson wear makeup in public.
TRUTH: All performers wear stage makeup, and certainly in videos. But offstage? Not!

RUMOR: Hanson are moving to . . . New Jersey . . . Florida . . . North Carolina . . . your town, USA.
TRUTH: Though fans would love to see the boys settle in their hometowns, the answer is no. Hanson isn't moving anywhere.

RUMOR: Hanson's coming out with Hanson dolls.
TRUTH: No doubt, they've been offered that by toy companies, but it's another suggestion they've politely nixed.

RUMOR: Hanson are doing a sitcom.
TRUTH: See above.

RUMOR: Zac will never put his hair in braids again, because girls try to pull at them.
TRUTH: Yes, girls have pulled at them, but with Zac, you never know.

RUMOR: Taylor was lip syncing in the "MMMBop" video.
TRUTH: No way! What would be the point anyway?

RUMOR: Zac threw up before a show because he didn't want to perform.
TRUTH: Like most people, Zac sometimes gets a tummy ache. But most often, it's from something he ate, or motion sickness, never from stage fright.

RUMOR: Tay's dating Liv Tyler, the actress.
TRUTH: Tay, and the rest of Hanson, met not only Liv [center] but the rest of Aerosmith lead singer Steven Tyler's family backstage in New York. That's Chelsea [left], and Mia [right], holding Taj. Meeting — and having their picture snapped together — does not exactly constitute dating!

Meeting Dick Clark was a total thrill for Ike, Zac, and Tay.

Chapter Eight

FAST FORWARD — WZUP?

It's been a Hanson world since they exploded onto the scene in 1997 and kept it great throughout '98. What's on the line for '99 and beyond?

For sure: Next for Hanson is a new album—technically their sixth—counting 1997's *Snowed In* Christmas album and 1998's repackaging of their two self-released CDs into *3 Car Garage: The Indie Recordings, '95-'96.*

They wish: "We would love to do other things," says Zac. Definition: producing records and writing songs for other people.

For Me:

This is what I know I'll be doing next year:_____

_____

This is what I hope I'll be doing:_____

_____

HANSON AWARDS

Nickelodeon Kids' Choice Awards: "Favorite Group" and "Favorite Song" ("MMMBop")
MTV European Award: "Best Pop Group"

YOUR HANSON AWARDS

Best Looking:
Cutest:
Most Talented:
Hanson Most Likely to Release a Solo Album:
Hanson Most Likely to Have a Girlfriend First:
Hanson Most Likely to Marry First:
Next Hanson Most Likely to Join the Band:

OTHER GROUPS THAT ARE POPULAR NOW

Backstreet Boys
Spice Girls
'N Sync

Chapter Nine

DISCOGRAPHY

ALBUMS
Boomerang
MMMBop
Middle of Nowhere
Snowed In
3 Car Garage: The Indie Recordings, '95-'96

SINGLES
"MMMBop"
"Where's the Love"
"I Will Come to You"
"Weird"
"The River"

LONG-FORM VIDEO
Tulsa, Tokyo, and the Middle of Nowhere

TV SPECIALS
Meet Hanson, ABC-TV
MTV—Live From the Ten Spot
Storytellers for VH1 — Save the Music: Hanson
(a benefit to raise money for music programs in the schools)

Isn't It Inventive?
Gloria Stuart, the 88-year-old actress from Titanic, "stars" in the newest Hanson video for "The River" — cool idea!

HOW TO REACH THEM

Snail Mail:

Hanson Fan Club, c/o Hitz List, PO Box 703136, Tulsa, OK 74170

Hanson, c/o Mercury Records, 11150 Santa Monica Blvd., Suite 1100, Los Angeles, CA 90025

Hanson
c/o Triune Music Group, 8322 Livingston Way, Los Angeles, CA 90046

Voice mail:
[918] 446-3979 This is a toll call — check with your parents first.

E-mail:
hansonfans@hansononline.com

Web sites:
www.hansonline.com

www.mercuryrecords.com/mercury/artists/hanson

www.hansonhitz.com

READ ALL ABOUT 'EM!
Hanson books by Scholastic!

Hanson: An Unauthorized Biography
Totally Taylor
Zac Attack!

47

With Love, from Ike, Tay, and Zac — Hanson's Message to Fans (from their official bio):
"We would like to thank our fans for giving us the amazing, life-changing opportunity to tour the world and play our music for more people than we ever thought possible. To those of you we have met, and to the many more we hope to meet in the future — best wishes to you always."

With Love from Me: My Message to Hanson: